Put Your Best Foot Forward

A Young Dancer's Guide to Life

BY SUKI SCHORER
and the SCHOOL OF AMERICAN BALLET

Illustrations by Donna Ingemanson

WORKMAN PUBLISHING • NEW YORK

Library of Congress Cataloging-in-Publication Data is available.

ISBN-13: 978-0-7611-3795-5
ISBN-10: 0-7611-3795-5

Workman books are available at special discounts when purchased in bulk for
premiums and sales promotions as well as for fund-raising or educational use.
Special editions or book excerpts can also be created to specification. For
details, contact the Special Sales Director at the address below.

Book design by Janet Parker and Vanessa Ray

Workman Publishing Company, Inc.
708 Broadway
New York, NY 10003-9555
www.workman.com

Printed in China
First printing October 2005

10 9 8 7 6 5 4 3 2 1

Contents

Special pullout poster follows page 96.

Author's Note

Zoe Dominic

Suki at work with George Balanchine in 1965.

Almost everything I know about ballet comes from my years of classes with George Balanchine. Almost everything I know about life, and how to live it, also comes from him—through his teaching and through the example that he set. As a teacher at the School of American Ballet, I pass on his dance principles to young students who are working as hard as they can to become professional dancers. His memory helps guide me as I work with the students, trying to show them how to dance, how to learn, and how to grow. The approach they take to learning ballet is the approach they take to life itself.

Mr. B—we all called him that—was (with Lincoln Kirstein) the founder of the School of American Ballet and of the New York City Ballet. It was my great, good fortune to have George Balanchine as my teacher, and to become a ballerina in his company and then a teacher in his school.

In this book, some students at the School and I are pleased to share with you some of what we learned from him.

—SUKI SCHORER

You have two feet to carry you far.

The world is waiting for you.

You'll leap to great heights!
You'll dazzle and shine!

AMAZING!

All that you need is to learn
how to dance.
And you can start right now.

PART ONE

Life is a dance— join in

When something needs doing
(like cleaning your room, for example)…

Strike like the cobra.

Gather energy, and then—strike fast!
Move with speed and aim and
purpose. (That sock under your
dresser never had a chance.)

Life is a dance—join in

9

When storms rage and waters rise…

Glide like the swan.

Remember who you are and be proud: chest lifted, neck lengthened, and elegance in every line. (Ignore your brother's comments! No ruffled feathers!)

Put your best foot forward

Life is a dance—join in

11

When days are gray, when your
shoulders slump and your feet drag,
take a deep breath and…

Stand tall.

You'll have a much
better view.

Put your best foot forward

Stand Like a Dancer:

✴ Weight forward

✴ Hips pulled up and over your legs

✴ Stomach pulled in

✴ Torso and back lengthened

✴ Chest lifted up, with shoulders down and back

✴ Shoulders over hips

✴ Face presented

✴ Eyes alive and alert

✴ And the top of your head reaching for the sky

Even when standing still, dancers are ready to take off.

13

Go gracefully as a dancer
throughout the day....

Be in control.

M ove with purpose
and poise.

Behave beautifully.

You can be gracious just by saying "please" and "thank you." Behave beautifully all the time, and it will come naturally when you're in the spotlight.

Make the world a prettier place....

Sparkle.

*L*ight up the world. Dance
with your heart and soul
(and you can smile, too).

17

Let your body sing.

M usic is the basis of dance:
take music into your heart.

Put your best foot forward

Life is a dance—join in

Find beauty in the smallest details.

The gently swaying branch of a weeping willow. The curves and bends of each finger on your hand.

21

Wonderful, big things are made from the littlest parts.

Many small details are needed to make a big, beautiful dance.

Put your best foot forward

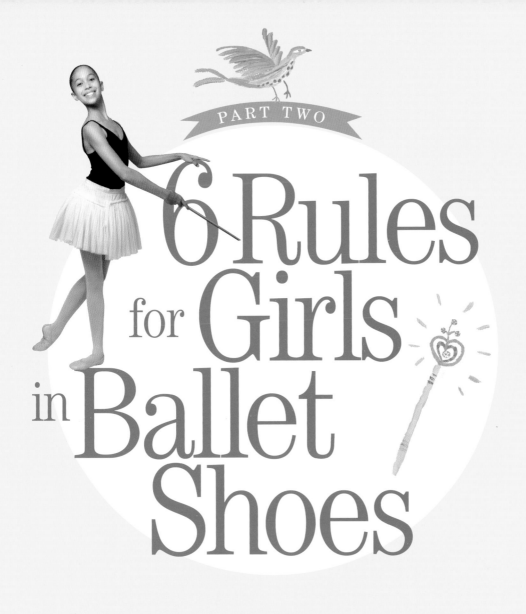

PART TWO

6 Rules
for Girls
in Ballet
Shoes

1. Be on time.

Be ready to move when it's time to go and start with energy. In dancing, being on time, being on the music, is the most important quality.

Don't miss a beat.

Put your best foot forward

2. Be precise.

Move with the same precision, whether you're moving fast or slow. Ballet classes always start slowly, and this gives you a chance to work on perfecting your movements. As the tempos get faster, try to hold on to what you've perfected. Stay in control, whatever the speed.

3. Lead a balanced life.

In first position, feel your center line. It starts where your heels meet, goes up through your body, past the belly button, up the middle of your chest, between your eyes, and on up to the sky.

To be balanced in arabesque, pull up on your supporting leg. Hold your abdominal muscles firmly as you lift your leg up against your back, while holding your back up.

Enjoy the stillness.

Put your best foot forward

4. Start on the right foot.

Picture a step before you take it. Get a clear picture in your mind of what you want your body to do. See yourself doing it. Then go for it—heart and soul, mind and body.

5. Always put your best foot forward.

Don't save your best dancing for tomorrow when you dance today. Give it everything, NOW!

6. Stay focused.

*L*earning requires your full attention. Don't lose sight of your goal. It may be closer than you think.

PART THREE

A Dancer is Always on Her Toes

Check that your skirt is on tight *before* you make an entrance.

A wet ribbon makes a stronger knot!

33

Be prepared!

A dancer's bag is a toolbox, medicine chest, suitcase, book bag, lunch box, and makeup kit.

Put your best foot forward

Keep Life's
Essentials Handy:

tights and leotard, ballet shoes, bobby pins
and clips, safety pins, needle and thread,
scissors, Band-Aids, hairbrush, snack,
bottle of water....

A dancer is always on her toes

Even a Sugar Plum Fairy sews her own ribbons.

Using a needle and thread is part of a dancer's life. Dancers need to sew elastics and ribbons on their own shoes and make repairs to their practice clothes.

Put your best foot forward

To Sew a Shoe:

1. Fold the heel down.
2. Sew the elastic or ribbon in place where the crease of the fold meets the side of the shoe.
3. Measure the correct length of elastic or ribbon.
4. Cut the elastic or ribbon to the correct length.
5. Sew the elastic firmly to the other side of the shoe.

Don't sew through the drawstring!

Put every hair in place.

Some like a high bun. Some like it low. Some do their hair in a twist. However you like it, practice a hairstyle until you master it, and you'll have freedom when you dance.

A dancer is always on her toes

Try on more shoes than you buy.

The right shoes are the ones in which you can dance well and that make your feet look their prettiest.

When Shopping
for Ballet Slippers:

look for soft kid leather.
It should be firm enough
to hold your foot and flexible
enough for a high *demi-pointe*.

Shoes

Take a chance.

Don't let fear hold you back. Falling down occasionally is part of learning. If you don't fall occasionally, your steps are probably too small and too careful. Mistakes are natural when you try anything new.

Put your best foot forward

Don't say you can't until you try, try, and try again.

You'll be surprised what you can do when you push yourself. Don't go to class expecting to feel safe and comfortable. A dancer must always reach beyond her safe place—and then a little beyond that.

Determination wins.

You will have setbacks. Sometimes it will seem you're going backward—not forward. Don't lose heart! Talent will take you only part of the way toward your goal. Most of a girl's ability comes from persistence and patience.

It takes a STRONG GIRL

PART FOUR

Be of Strong Mind and Body

to make beauty and magic....

Your body is your instrument.

Take good care of it.

- ✔ Feed your body when it's hungry.

- ✔ Give it a rest when it's tired.

- ✔ Exercise and go to ballet class to build your strength.

- ✔ Dance to make you and your body happy.

Be of strong mind and body

47

Be like the boa constrictor— flexible and powerful.

Flexibility allows you to throw your leg high. Strength lets you hold it there. Stretch every day after your muscles are warm.

Be of strong mind and body   49

Be patient.

Learning to dance is like planting a carrot seed. You weed and you water and you just see green leaves. But all the while, the carrot is growing underground. In ballet class, you work every day and you might think nothing is changing. But inside, you are getting stronger. The effort you put forward today may not show results tomorrow. But one day soon, it will. You'll see! You'll get your carrot!

Be of strong mind and body

51

Enjoy every step, every step of the way.

Don't wait for things to be perfect to enjoy yourself. Most of life is spent learning and preparing. Finishing, winning, and reaching the goal are just the last moments. Enjoy the dance from beginning to end.

Put your best foot forward

Be of strong mind and body   53

It takes strong wings to fly.

Eat your spinach.

Some things you may not like
are good for you: like eating
certain vegetables or practicing *tendus*. Work on the things
you do least well—not just
what you do best or enjoy doing.
Practicing every day builds a
strong technique. Eating properly
builds a healthy body.

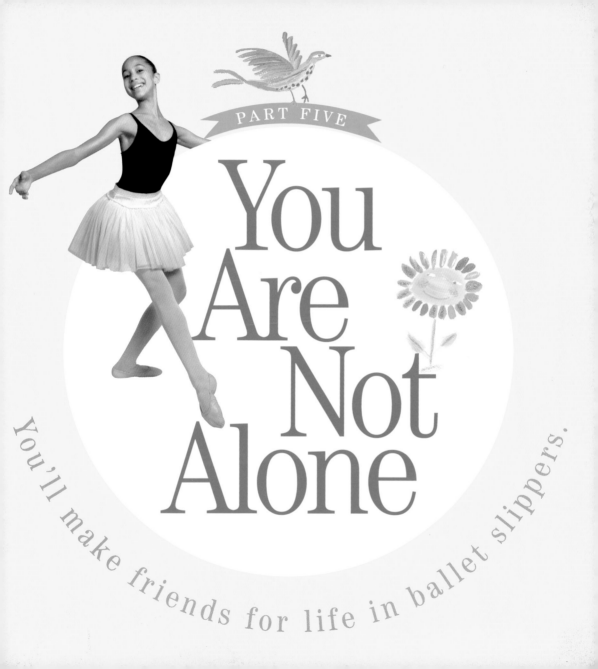

PART FIVE

You Are Not Alone

You'll make friends for life in ballet slippers.

Be a dancing tree in the forest.

*I*t's wonderful to dance with others. Together, you can make make more beautiful shapes and patterns than you could just dancing alone. When working as a team, each dancer shares in the effort; each dancer shares in the result.

You are not alone

Cheer for others.

*L*et people know when they do something wonderful.

Put your best foot forward

You are not alone

59

Lend a gentle touch.

Sometimes just a touch is all the support a person needs. The lightest touch can make the strongest bond.

You are not alone

61

Find a good partner.

Choose a partner who is capable, who is a good match for you, and with whom you feel comfortable. Partners need to work together to coordinate their timing and movements.

You are not alone

63

The boy needs to feel the girl's balance.
The girl must maintain her center.

Put your best foot forward

Learn how to learn.

A teacher can guide, suggest, and correct. But only *you* can actually do. Put into practice today everything you learned yesterday, and you'll continue to grow.

Put your best foot forward

Be grateful for criticism.

There is always room for improvement. Be receptive and thankful.

You can't learn to do everything all by yourself.

Never take the things you love for granted.

When you make a *révérence* at the end of class, you are thanking the teacher and the pianist, and expressing your deep respect for the art of ballet and its traditions. The teacher's bow in return expresses her respect and gratitude.

This art we love so much was developed and passed on to us from teacher to dancer over hundreds of years—from one generation to the next.

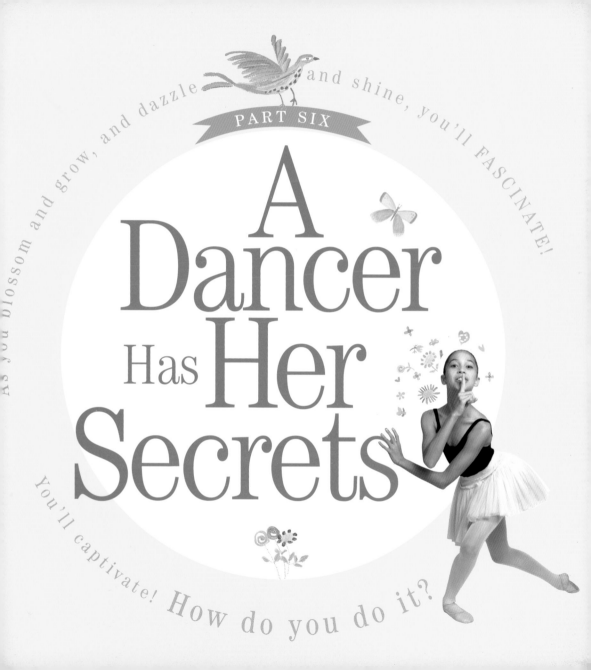

PART SIX

As you blossom and grow, and dazzle and shine, you'll FASCINATE!

A Dancer Has Her Secrets

You'll captivate! How do you do it?

Generate power!

In ballet class, you gather power as you *plié*. When you bend your knees in a *plié*, it is like compressing a spring. Feel the resistance as you bend. You are collecting energy for the next movement. *Plié* provides the energy for a jump and the control as you land. The landing *plié* is a shock absorber for your entire body and supplies energy for the next movement.

A dancer has her secrets

71

Bring joy.

Bring joy when you dance— to yourself and to others. Forget your cares and worries! Be generous. Give it everything you have. It's just you and the music and the dance.

A dancer has her secrets

73

Step Lightly.

Land on the floor delicately,
like a mother bird landing on
her eggs.

The ground is your friend.
The air is your home.

Put your best foot forward

A dancer has her secrets

Speak loudest when you're silent.

Express yourself with your whole body. Show each movement so that the gesture is clear and precise.

Be dramatic.

Be gone!

Out!
Out!
Out!

Away with you!

A dancer has her secrets

A look can say more than a word.

Speak with your body as beautifully as dappled sunlight on flower petals.

Put your best foot forward

Be poetic.

I can be mysterious.

Make people look your way.

irect your audience. Look down to announce that your foot is leaving the floor. Look over your hand and toward your foot to show the audience that you lifted it. Use your eyes to direct people to see what you want them to see.

Put your best foot forward

Do something extraordinary
just because you can....

Dance on air.

Earth's gravity is no match for a
dancer. Hold a position as long
as you can to give the illusion
that you are floating in space.

A dancer has her secrets

Imagine.

Life should be a moving
experience: bring your
movements to life by using
your imagination.

Put your best foot forward

Look under your arm as though you could see the moon in the sky.

A dancer has her secrets

tand with your arms in first position. Take a breath of fresh air and expand your chest— imagine that you smell a sweet morning breeze. Open your arms wide. Gently pull your shoulder blades together and open your chest. Use the muscles at the sides of your body, holding your arms as if they were floating on air.

As you move your arms from first to second, part th

Hug a big tree in first position.

Put your best foot forward

See yourself at a *magnificent party.* Look over your arm as if you were looking over the rail of a grand balcony.

...rtains on a beautiful, new morning.

Step into the spotlight.

Announce yourself with a powerful presence.

A dancer has her secrets

Accept applause graciously.

Applause means, "Thank you." A curtsy means "You're very welcome!" A quick run offstage means, "Bye for now!"

A dancer has her secrets

Be yourself.

My teacher said it takes many kinds of flowers to make a beautiful garden: many kinds of dancers to make an interesting dance. You are a flower who'll bloom your own way. You are unique and special.

PART SEVEN

You are on your way

A girl who dances can dance through Life.

Y ou'll have strength and balance to follow your heart. And, wherever you go, you'll have grace to make each movement a dance.

All your efforts in learning to dance—the discipline, focus, and concentration—will be yours forever to make a beautiful life, no matter where your feet take you.

You are on your way

You'll be

AMAZING!

You will go far.